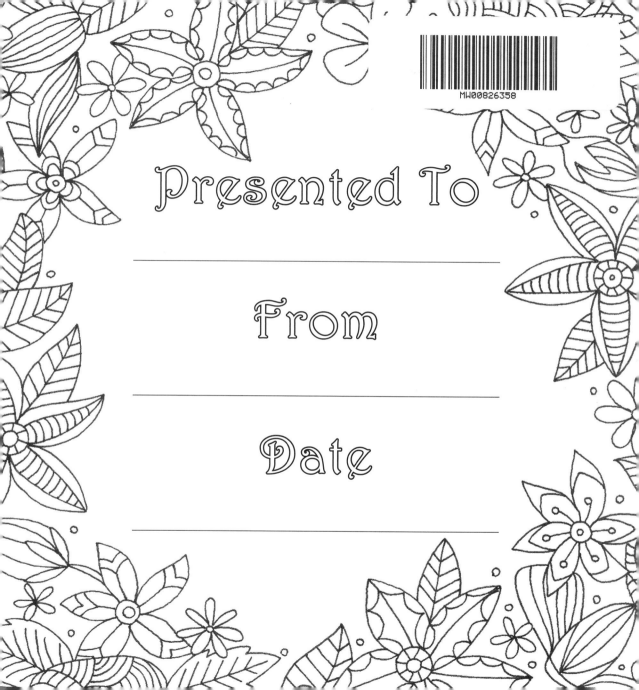

Presented To

_____

From

_____

Date

_____

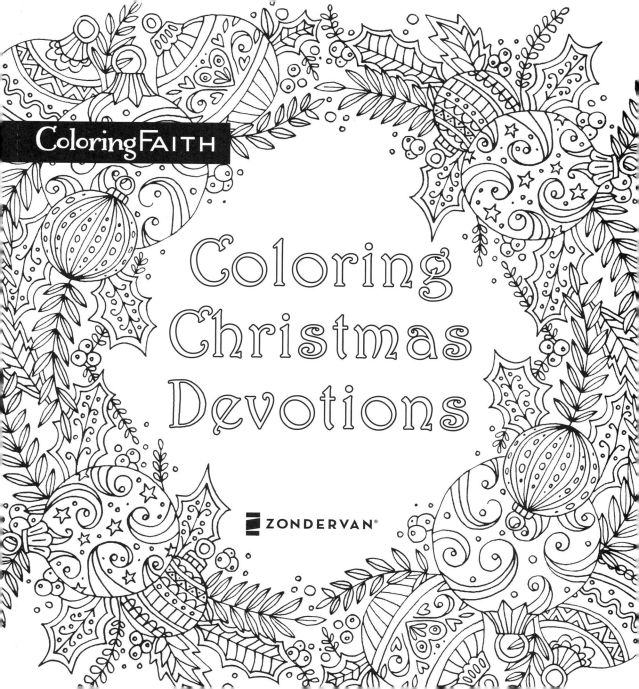

Coloring FAITH

Coloring
Christmas
Devotions

ZONDERVAN®

Coloring Christmas Devotions

Copyright © 2017 by Zondervan

Requests for information should be addressed to:
Zondervan, 3900 Sparks Dr., SE, Grand Rapids, MI 49546

ISBN 978-0-310-08809-7

Cover design: Patti Evans
Interior design: Mallory Collins

Printed in the United States

17 18 19 20 21 LSC 22 21 20 19 18 17 16 15 14 13 12 11 10 9 8 7 6 5 4 3 2 1

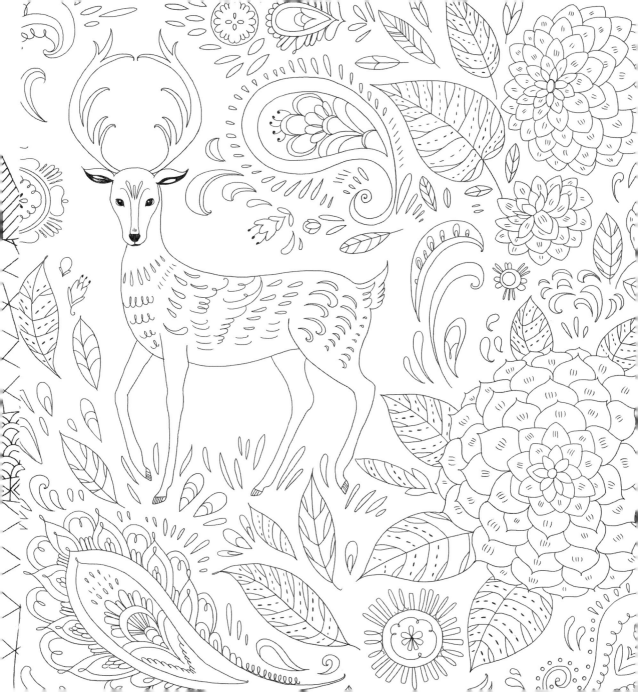

Surprise Packaging

Hariett has a real gift when it comes to gift wrapping. She's given concert tickets tucked inside empty cereal boxes and jewelry disguised in old coffee cans. Hariett takes great joy in surprising people with offbeat packaging, and they never guess what's inside. What about you? Do you judge presents by the packaging? Have you ever been surprised by what was inside?

The children of Israel were anticipating the coming of the Messiah, and they had a certain image in their minds. They were awaiting the arrival of a military leader who would show up on the scene with a lot of fanfare. They were expecting someone who would demand attention and respect by his very presence. Can you imagine their confusion when the Christ Child made His humble entrance into the world?

From the very beginning, Christmas has been about precious gifts in unexpected packaging. The Son of God entered our world clothed in the flesh of an infant. God's plan to redeem and restore His people began with a newborn's cry. It was the ultimate surprise gift.

Scripture is full of gifts from God that are wrapped in mysterious ways. From the heart of a king hidden inside a shepherd boy to the Messiah in a manger to angels disguised as strangers, God is full of beautiful surprises. It's so easy to get caught up in appearances. But when we do, we can miss out on the best gifts. Let's ask God to open our eyes to the beautiful surprises that are all around us.

I am so thankful, Lord, that You came the way You did. Thank You for teaching us to see beyond the wrapping to the beautiful gift inside. Amen.

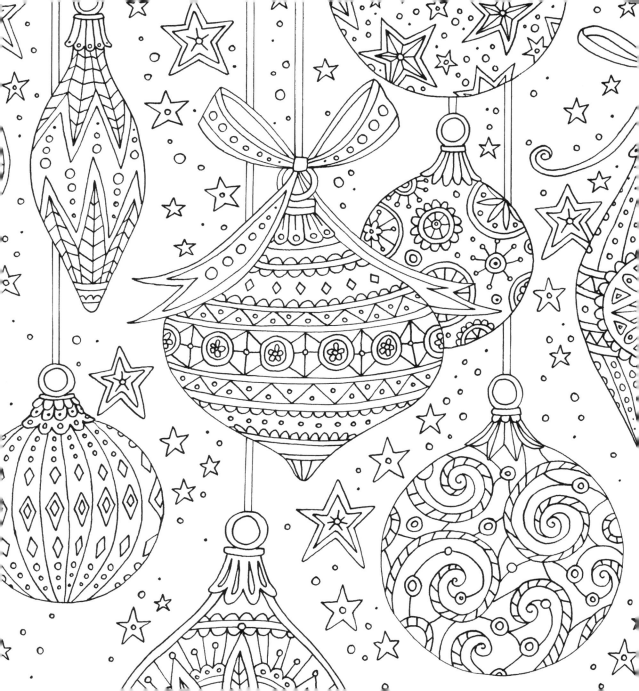

Therefore the LORD himself will give you a sign. Behold, the virgin shall conceive and bear a SON, and shall call his name *Immanuel.*

—ISAIAH 7:14

Heavenly Peace

*Glory to God in the highest heaven, and on
earth peace to those on whom his favor rests.*
—LUKE 2:14 NIV

Let's face it: Christmas can be stressful. We get caught up in trying to create the perfect holiday. We worry about family members not getting along or the mashed potatoes being lumpy. Before we know it, we're longing for a little of the peace we hear about in Christmas carols.

When Christmas rolled around in 1914, World War I was in full swing. Though Pope Benedict XV suggested a temporary cease-fire in honor of the holiday, the warring countries refused to make it official. Peace did not seem anywhere in sight.

When the holiday arrived, the soldiers themselves chose to lay down their weapons in honor of Christmas. It was the first reprieve in months: the sound of gunfire was replaced with the sound of singing. Enemies were reported to have exchanged gifts and played games. Though the war was far from over, the Christmas Truce of 1914 brought a little peace amid the conflict.

What conflict are you dealing with this Christmas? Family drama, financial struggles, or a health concern? No matter the circumstance, Christ has promised His peace to you. Peace is always available for those of us who love Him. Our holidays do not have to be marked by stress and conflict. Let's take Christmas back. This year, let's choose peace.

No peace is found in accomplishments, popularity, or wealth. True peace is only found in Your presence, Jesus. Thank You, Lord, for the peace of Christmas. Amen.

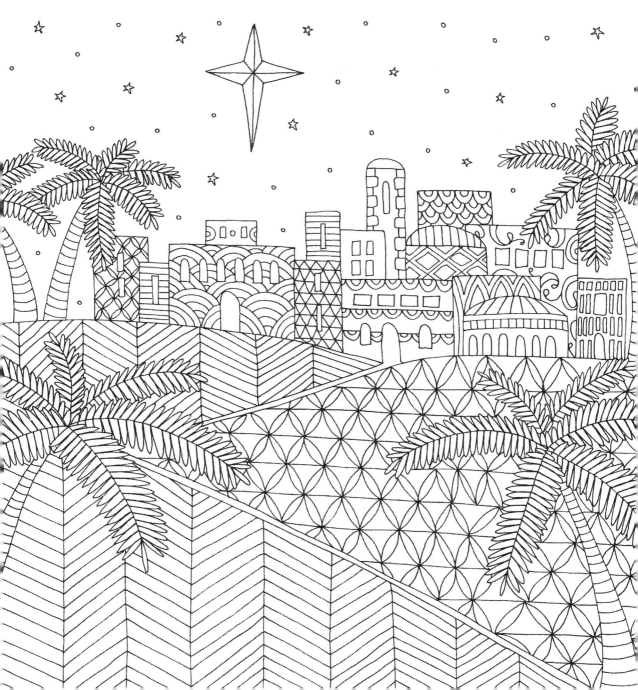

Family Traditions

Jesus Christ is the same yesterday and today and forever.
—Hebrews 13:8 niv

Have you ever seen the movie *Christmas with the Kranks*? When faced with a loss of traditions, the Krank family takes drastic measures and cancels Christmas!

We might not go to such extremes, but we all have traditions that are near and dear to our hearts. The familiar smell of cider on the stove or the sound of a favorite Christmas carol can bring warmth and comfort to our holiday. What traditions make your holiday season? Now imagine someone changing your tried-and-true recipe or suggesting a new location for the holiday meal. Our traditions bring us such stability and peace that any change can sting. We might be like the Kranks and feel like giving up altogether!

For those of us who find comfort in consistency, there is good news. Our holidays may not always look the same, but the Jesus whom we celebrate will never change. Jesus will always be who He has always been. Scripture shows us that Jesus has been consistent in His compassion, His character, and His commands. James said that Christ "does not change like shifting shadows" (James 1:17 niv).

Traditions are meaningful and create beautiful memories for our families, but perhaps we can be more flexible this year. We could leave a little room for the inevitable changes of life. This may mean loosening our grip on Grandma's sweet potato pie recipe and letting that be okay. Who knows what new joy may come along with change? Let's make this Christmas the year we choose Christ over our traditions.

Thank You, Lord, for the consistency of Christmas and for the Child we celebrate. In a world where feelings fade and people change, Christmas is a beautiful reminder of the Savior who is always the same. Amen.

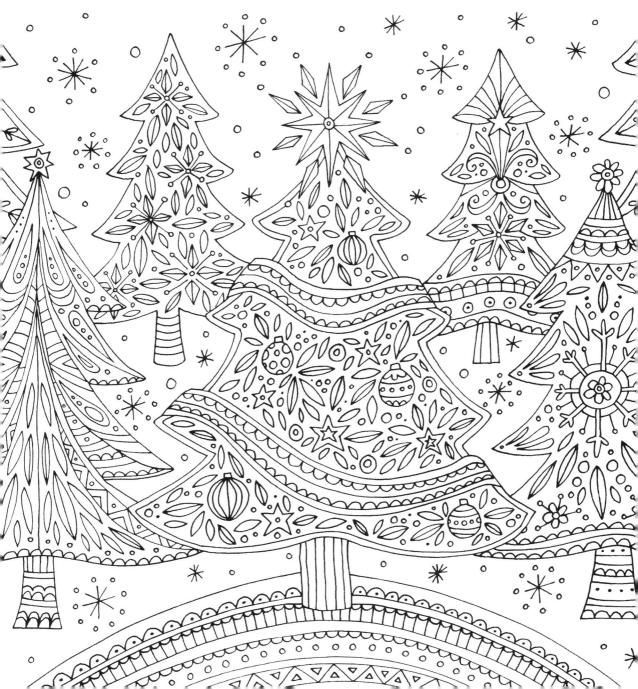

The voice of one crying in the wilderness: "Prepare the way of the LORD; Make straight in the desert A highway for our GOD. Every valley shall be exalted And every MOUNTAIN and hill brought low;The crooked places shall be made straightAnd the rough places SMOOTH; The GLORY of the LORD shall be revealed."

—ISAIAH 40:3–5 NKJV

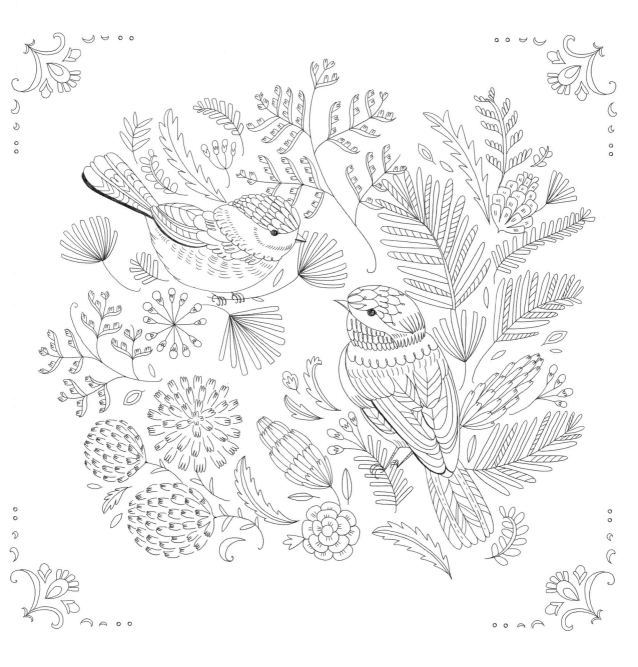

Pure as New Snow

You were ransomed . . . with the precious blood of Christ,
like that of a lamb without blemish or spot.
—1 PETER 1:18–19

What is your immediate thought when snow falls for the first time each year? For some of us, our instinct is to rush outside and gather that fresh, pure snow; bring it inside; and add a little vanilla, milk, and sugar. If done correctly, the end result is the winter treat *snow cream*. If you aren't familiar with snow cream, there is one hard-and-fast rule: only the purest snow will do.

All throughout the Old Testament, people sought purity—to be made as clean as new snow. The psalmist pleaded to God, "Purify me from my sins, and I will be clean; wash me, and I will be whiter than snow" (Psalm 51:7 NLT). God's people performed sacrifices in an attempt to be right with Him. They offered lambs, doves, or whatever the Law prescribed for their situation. The problem was that these offerings were only temporary. Because the animals were imperfect sacrifices, another sacrifice would soon be needed to cover new sins. A pure offering simply wasn't available.

Fortunately, God always had a plan for the redemption of His people and for a pure and perfect sacrifice: His Son. Christ was not just a precious baby. He was the Lamb without spot or blemish. He came to be the sacrifice once and for all because only a completely pure offering would make us right with God.

This Christmas, let's remember why Jesus came and give our thanks to Him. The cradle was always about the cross. As we think about Jesus as a baby, let's not be afraid to look ahead to His purpose in coming. Christ came because only a totally pure sacrifice would do.

Jesus, thank You for being the perfect sacrifice. Thank You for doing for us what we could not do for ourselves. Amen.

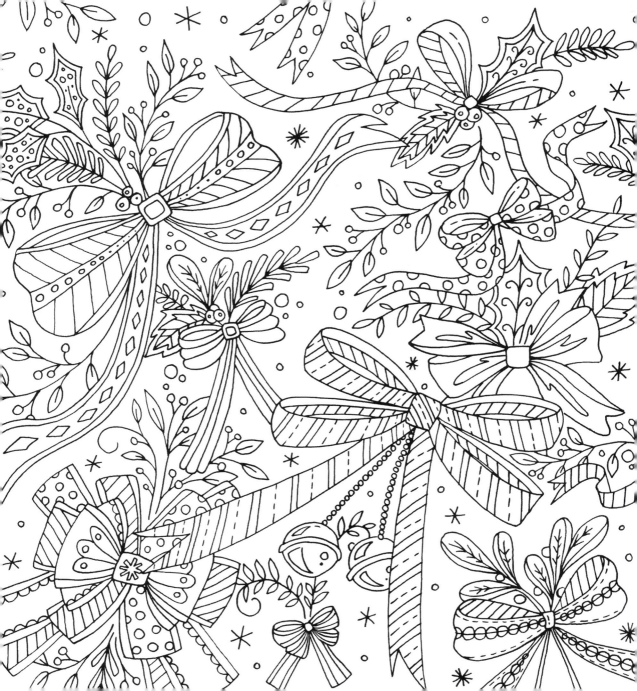

An Ordinary Christmas

In the same region there were shepherds out in the field,
keeping watch over their flock by night.
—LUKE 2:8

Isn't Christmas the perfect time to flex a little creative muscle? Dreams of sugarplum-frosted trees and perfect parties fill our heads. We plot and plan the perfect gifts. We outdo ourselves with new cookie recipes and leaf through magazines, looking for spectacular displays to re-create at home. As we attempt to pull together something extraordinary, we may spend a great deal of money, time, and energy on all the details. Creating an impressive Christmas can be exhausting, but let's remember that beauty can be found in an ordinary celebration of Christmas too.

After all, it was just an ordinary night for the shepherds in Bethlehem. Then, right in the middle of their usual grazing land and their normal evening, angels appeared, proclaiming the birth of the Savior. God invaded the shepherds' regular night with His holiness, and they were never the same.

We do not need to create something extraordinary for God to show up. He sent angels to shepherds in a field. Zechariah, a priest, was performing his duties in the temple when the angel Gabriel appeared to him. Jesus' first disciples were fishing when He called them to follow Him. God shows Himself to ordinary people who are doing ordinary things. He knows where to find us, and when He does, beautiful things happen.

We all want our holidays to be special, but special does not have to be stressful. It's perfectly fine to crave a little ordinary in our celebration this Christmas. Let's gather around a fireplace with some hot cocoa and thank God for the beauty that is found in an ordinary life.

We do not need to create a spectacle to catch Your attention, Lord. Faithfulness is what You seek. Help us find Your beauty in the ordinary. Amen.

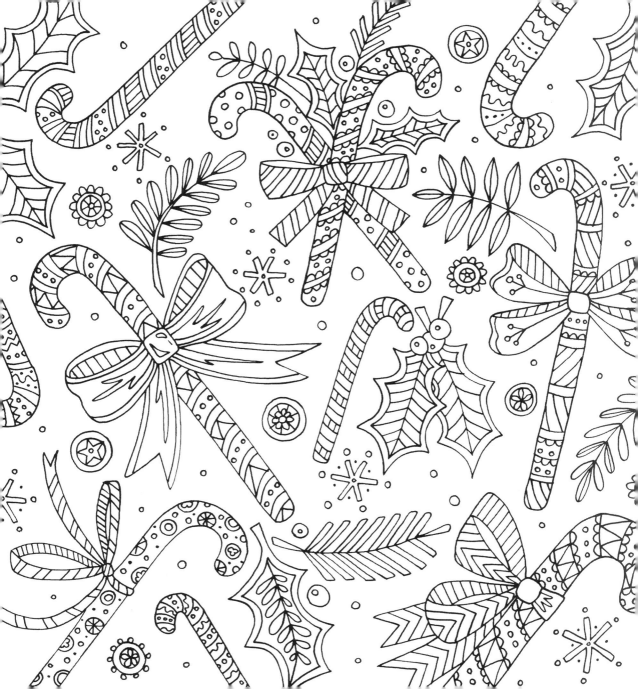

Rejoice greatly, O daughter of Zion!

Shout, O daughter of Jerusalem!

Behold, your *King* is coming to you;

He is just and having salvation,

Lowly and RIDING on a donkey,

A colt, the foal of a donkey.

—ZECHARIAH 9:9 NKJV

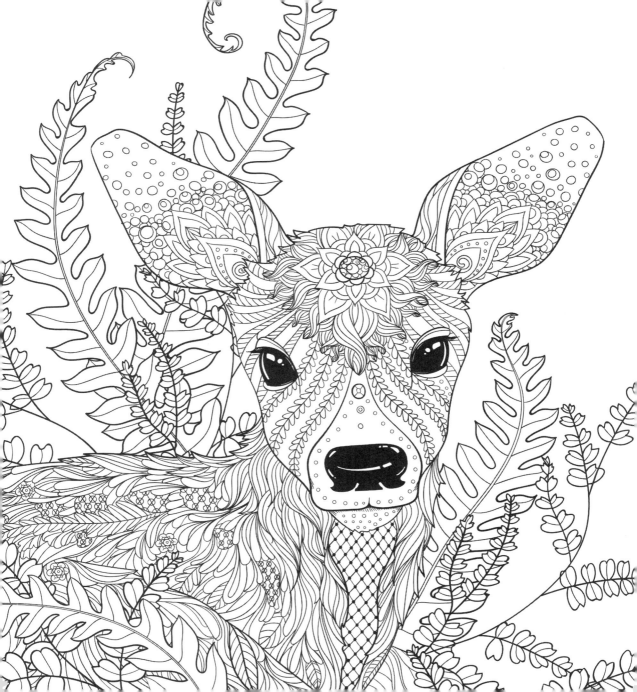

Saving Room for Dessert

When they had brought their boats to land, they left everything and followed him.
—LUKE 5:11

Sitting at Christmas dinner, you can find it hard to believe that one more helping of mashed potatoes could ever be a bad idea. But at some point you realize it can be—usually right about the time someone asks you if you saved room for dessert. Those potatoes were good, but some pumpkin pie would have been better. Metaphorically speaking, have you ever overindulged and, as a result, missed out on something better?

When Jesus called His first disciples, they were busy living their lives. Luke 5 describes a group of fishermen—disappointed by a poor catch—who were washing their nets. After Jesus taught the multitudes standing on the shore, He told the disciples to cast their nets again—and the nets came up completely full! The fishermen could have stayed, made a lot of money at market, and filled their bellies for some time. But they would have missed out on the far greater blessing of walking with the Savior. They made the wise decision and "left everything and followed him."

We all have certain things that give us the illusion of fulfillment. We may think that wealth or fame or a certain relationship will bring us satisfaction. If we aren't careful, we will fill ourselves with the things of this world when God has far better things in store. Gorging on the world's offerings can leave us wishing we had chosen more wisely. After all, the way of Christ never leads to regret. As we pick and choose what we put on our plates this day, may we carefully consider whether each thing brings true fulfillment.

Teach us to wait patiently for You, Lord. May we not fill ourselves with the things of this world. Give us an appetite for the things of God. Amen.

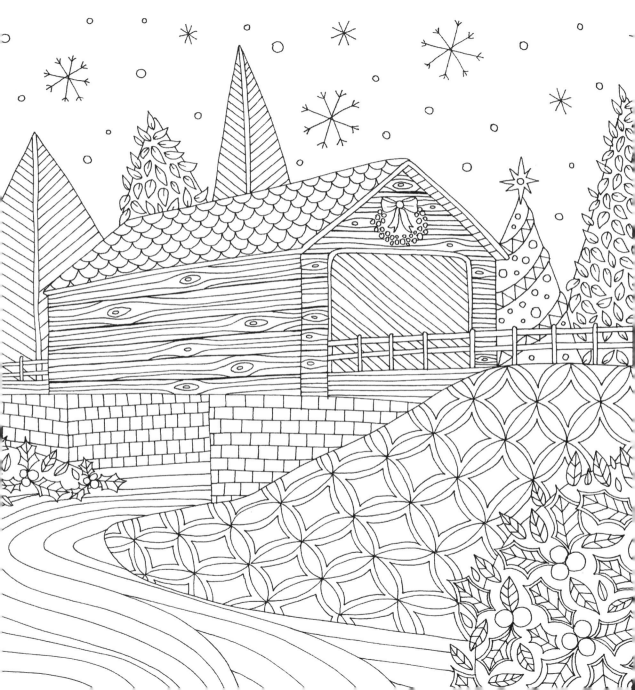

Christmas Lights

When they saw the star, they rejoiced exceedingly with great joy.
—MATTHEW 2:10

One family in New York holds the Guinness World Record title for the most lights in a residential Christmas display: this family hangs more than six hundred thousand lights. People drive from miles around to see the fantastic display glowing in the night.

What kind of Christmas light displays bring out the kid in you? Multicolored or white? Big bulbs, little bulbs, or icicles? Blinking or not? Twinkling lights add plenty of cheer to the dark, cold nights of winter. In fact, the very first Christmas began with a light shining in the sky. When the wise men in a distant country saw the star, they referred to it as "his star" (Matthew 2:2) because many years earlier a prophet had prophesied that a star would announce the birth of a king (Numbers 24:17). Actually, from the very beginning God has been dispelling darkness both literally and in our hearts.

What areas of darkness do you struggle with? We all have secrets or pain that we try to keep hidden. We may think it is better not to show our struggles, but the truth is that shame flourishes in the dark. Furthermore, God wants us, His people, to walk in the light. This is why Jesus refers to Himself as the light of the world (John 8:12).

Let's be like the wise men this Christmas and seek the light of Christ. Let's open up to God about our most personal troubles and receive His healing and hope. We were never meant to live in darkness, and Christmas is the perfect time to leave our darkness behind. When you're putting up lights this year, hang an extra strand to remind you that God's light chases away the darkness.

The dark is no place for Your people, Lord. Thank You for shining Your light into our lives so we can see another way. Amen.

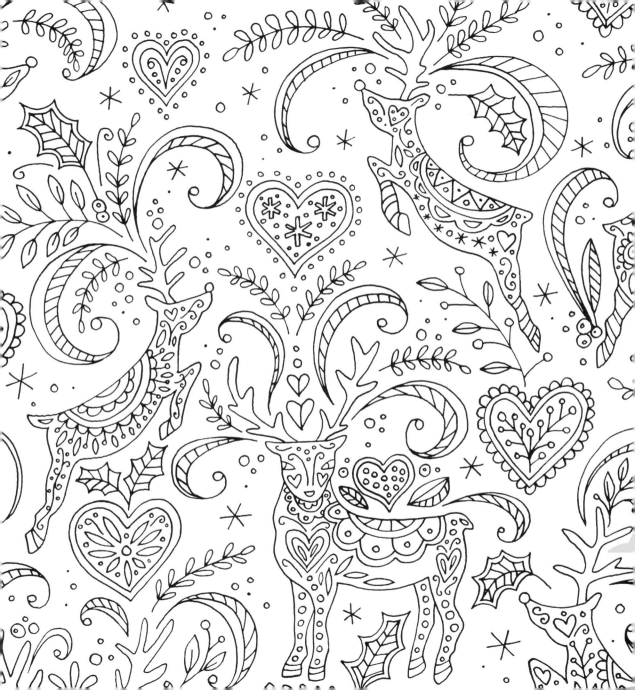

An Unexpected Gift

*It has been given to you on Christ's behalf not only
to believe in Him, but also to suffer for Him.*
—Philippians 1:29 HCSB

According to a January 2015 *Time* magazine article, Britain's royal family receives an odd assortment of gifts each year. Some of the most unusual were twelve boxes of mangos for Prince Andrew, a PhD thesis for Charles and Camilla, and even a pair of giant turtles for Queen Elizabeth. What is the most surprising gift you have received? Have you ever opened a present and thought, *What in the world were they thinking?*

When we accept Christ as Savior and choose to follow Him, we also receive gifts—but they are perfectly suited for us and for God's plan for us. We are promised His peace, comfort, and joy. We have the gift of His presence and guidance. There are innumerable blessings in following Him. Yet we are also promised trials and tribulation. According to Paul, we receive the gifts of both believing and suffering.

Whether we are serving or suffering, we get to do it for Christ. That is a gift. Are we ever closer to Him than during a time of suffering? Pastor and teacher John Piper said it this way: "There is more of God to be had in times of suffering than any other time." And who wouldn't want more of God?

None of us wants to ask God for suffering. It is certainly nothing that we would add to our Christmas wish lists. Yet if we walk with Christ, suffering will come. Let's pray that we will accept suffering with thankful hearts when it comes, knowing that God will work it out for His glory.

Suffering is an unexpected gift, and it scares us, Lord. Give us whatever we need to endure faithfully and in a way that honors You. Amen.

Home for the Holidays

Joseph also went up from Galilee, from the town of Nazareth, to Judea, to the city of David, which is called Bethlehem, because he was of the house and lineage of David.
—Luke 2:4

The days leading up to Christmas are some of the busiest travel days of the year. Soon the roads will be filled with people heading home for the holiday. We will load up the car and make the journey, knowing that home waits at the other end.

What sights and sounds say "home" to you? For many of us, Christmas is Mama's macaroni salad. It is listening to Dad's story about that time he was stuck in Detroit on Christmas Day because of a snowstorm. We go home for the holidays because where we come from is part of who we are.

The days leading up to the birth of Christ found Joseph and his family traveling home to Bethlehem. All the people had to return to their hometowns for a census, which was being conducted just in time for Jesus' birth. Where Joseph came from and, ultimately, where Jesus came from mattered in the grand plan of God. Jesus' birthplace fulfilled prophecies that the Messiah would be from the house of David and that He would be born in Bethlehem. Joseph's return home was a perfectly orchestrated part of God's plan.

Home is different things for different people. Perhaps you don't have fond memories of smoked turkey and handmade gifts, but where you come from still matters. God dreamed up every detail of you before you were born, and He is working your origins, your past, your present, and your future together as part of His grand plan. And if Christ is your Savior, your future includes a journey to a new, eternal home in heaven. We can spend this holiday looking heavenward in our hearts, knowing one day we will all truly be home for the holidays.

One day, Lord, we will all be home in Your presence. We long for that glad reunion day, and we thank You for guiding our lives as we get there. Amen.

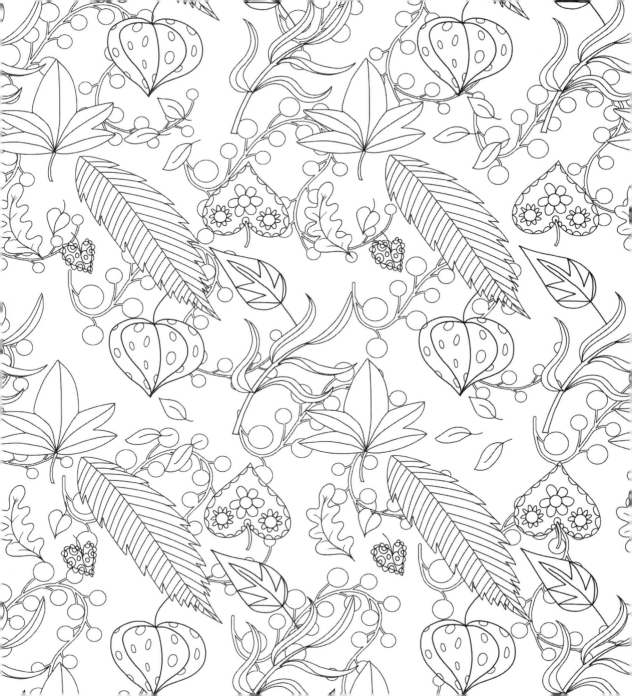

The angel said to her, "Do not be afraid, Mary, for you have found *favor* with God. And behold, you will conceive in your womb and bear a son, and you will call his name JESUS. He will be *great* and will be called the Son of the Most High. And the LORD GOD will give him the throne of his father David, and he will reign over the house of Jacob *forever*, and of his kingdom there will be no end."

—LUKE 1:30–33

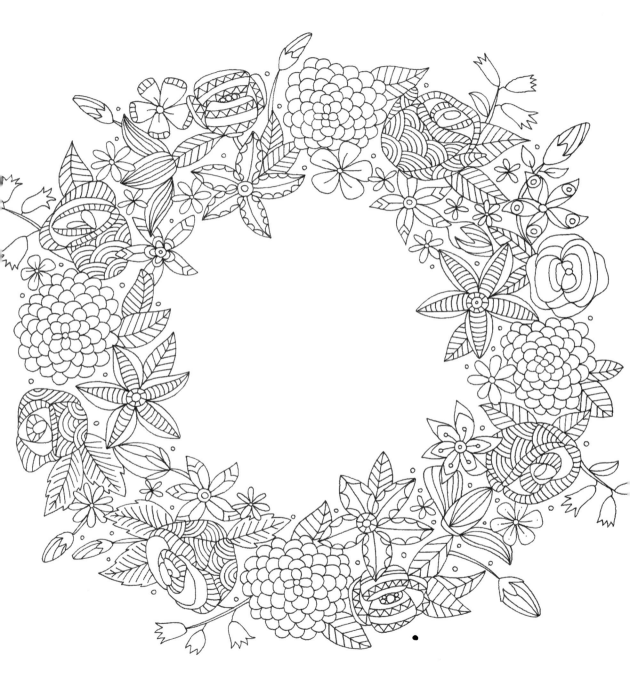

Seated at the Table

One of the Pharisees asked [Jesus] to eat with him, and he
went into the Pharisee's house and reclined at the table.
—LUKE 7:36

Would you be surprised to know that a traditional Christmas meal in the Czech Republic includes fried carp? If you were invited to a holiday meal in Peru, you would probably find a roast turkey stuffed with ground beef and peanuts. For most of us, the Christmas dinner menu is sacred. We want to see Mama's chestnut stuffing and Aunt Dee's red velvet cake just as we do every year. Much planning and preparation go into Christmas dinner, and for the most part, nobody wants any surprises.

Throughout Christ's ministry He was often seated at a table, dining with a surprising variety of individuals. People have always mattered to Him, so the most important part of any meal was not what was served on the table but who was seated at the table. When the sinful woman interrupted the Pharisee's meal to wash Jesus' feet with a fragrant oil (Luke 7), Christ welcomed her without hesitation because she mattered more than custom or tradition did.

Perhaps people in our circles of influence are changing the way Christmas decorating and activities have always been done and upsetting the comfort and calm of the traditional and familiar. Will we, like Jesus, offer those people a seat at our Christmas table? This hypothetical situation may be literal: with new faces, new dishes, or new circumstances, our holiday meals look different than they did in years past. Or maybe these thoughts are significant on a figurative level, and our attitudes must change so we will value people's hearts more than we value the traditions we cling to. Let's welcome interruptions without hesitation and not be afraid to make room at the table this Christmas.

Forgive us, Lord, for making our plans more of a priority than we make people. Send people our way, and we will offer them a seat at our table. Amen.

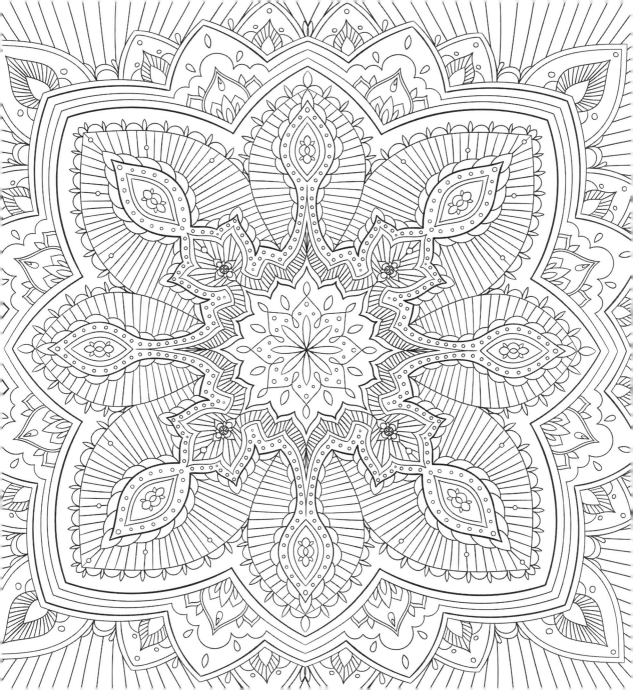

Hot Apple Cider

"Let not your hearts be troubled. Believe in God; believe also in me."
—JOHN 14:1

T hink about when you have faced particularly trying times. What brought comfort to your soul? What are some little things that warmed your heart? During this winter season, not many things bring comfort like a cup of hot apple cider. The smell of it simmering on the stove and the feel of the warm mug in our hands make our hearts happy. That comfort is never more needed than when we have been out in the cold.

We all go through times in our lives when we experience loss and heartache, and the world seems a little colder. For many people the holidays can be challenging because the special times remind them of what and whom they've lost. While we may try to cheer them up or make things better, Christ is the true Source of comfort. He is the One who can bring true warmth into a chilly world.

When Jesus spoke the words in John 14:1, He was comforting His disciples after informing them that He would be leaving. They were focusing on their loss, but He wanted them to focus on Him. Similarly, we can take comfort during the coldest season by keeping our gaze on Christ and on the hope of resurrection and restoration. Paul referred to God as the God of all comfort (2 Corinthians 1:3), and He is still that for us today.

Think about people you know. Who needs comfort this Christmas? Maybe you do. Let's remind ourselves and those around us that Christ is the ultimate Source of comfort. May His mercy and compassion flow through us in our prayers, in sympathetic words, and in small acts of love. Hot apple cider is never a bad idea either.

You, Lord, bring warmth and comfort in the midst of a cold world. Teach us to turn to You and be warmed by Your love. Amen.

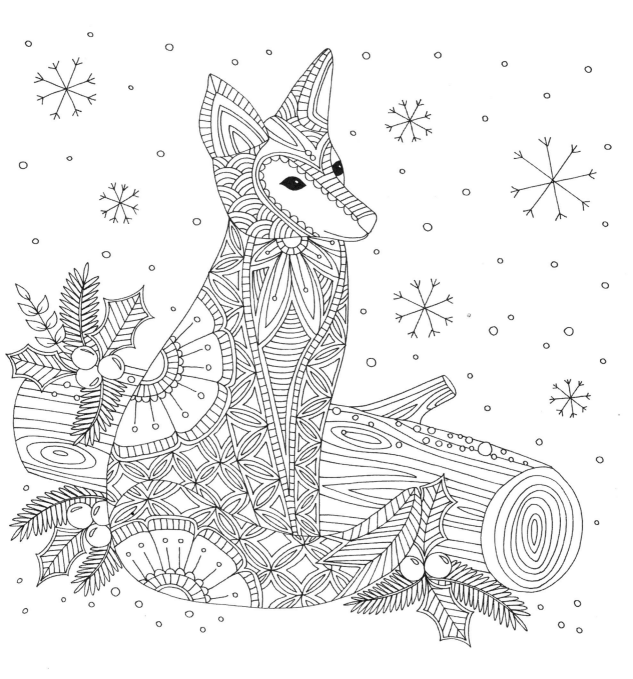

[Elizabeth] spoke out with a loud voice and said, "BLESSED are you among women, and blessed is the fruit of your womb! But why is this granted to me, that the mother of my Lord should come to me? For indeed, as soon as the voice of your greeting sounded in my ears, the babe leaped in my womb for joy. Blessed is she who believed, for there will be a FULFILLMENT of those things which were told her from the Lord."

—Luke 1:42–45 NKJV

Unwrapping the Mystery

Beyond all question, the mystery from which true
godliness springs is great: He appeared in the flesh.
—1 TIMOTHY 3:16 NIV

The days leading up to Christmas are full of mystery and excitement. Packages of all shapes and sizes sit under the tree. Small treasures stick out of the tops of stockings. Children try to guess what each present holds. Most adults are content to let the suspense remain a little longer. What about you? Do you enjoy surprises? Do you—like the children—want to know what is in each box, or are you happy to let the mystery last?

On more than one occasion, Paul referred to Christ and the gospel as a mystery. One of the greatest aspects of this mystery is that God would put on flesh and live among us. This was certainly not the way God's people had envisioned the coming of the Messiah. Yet it was exactly how He needed to come in order to ransom His people. We received the very thing we didn't even know we needed—because God alone knew the only way to rescue us from our sin.

The mystery of Christ is still being unwrapped. We only know part of His work on earth and a portion of His plan for humanity, but one day all will be revealed (1 Corinthians 13:12). While it's tempting to want to know all the answers, why not embrace the wonder of it all? There are some things we are not meant to know, and that's okay. After all, God's "understanding has no limit," while ours certainly does (Psalm 147:5 NIV). We can study, question, and seek answers, but let's not lose the wonder of God's infinitely transcendent plan. Rest in God's perfect timing. There is no need to rush things. He will finish unwrapping the mystery of Christ's coming, and we will be overwhelmed with joy.

We long to know every part of You, Lord, but You are more than our human minds can comprehend. Teach us to seek You and to lose ourselves in the mystery of You. Amen.

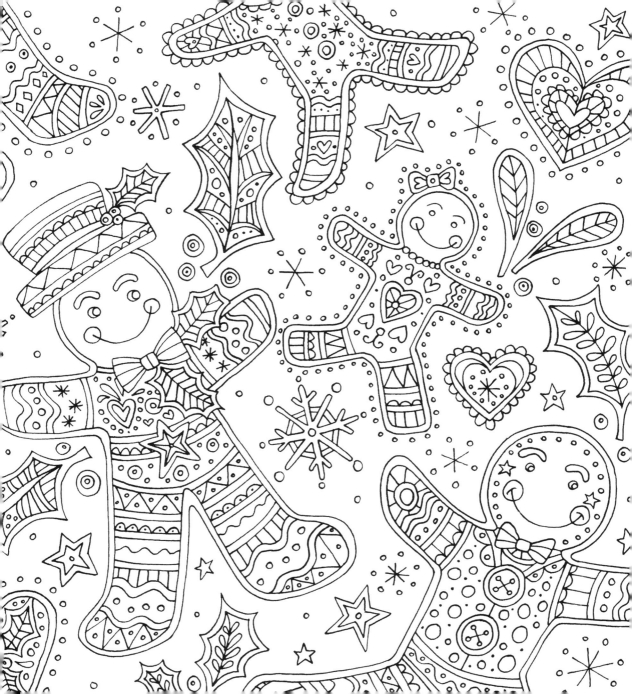

A Christmas List

All the promises of God find their Yes in him.
—2 CORINTHIANS 1:20

The United States Postal Service receives millions of letters addressed to Santa each year—and that's a lot of children asking for things they might not receive. Do you remember making a Christmas list as a kid? Every television commercial and store flyer had us running to add just one more item. Nothing seems off-limits for a child at Christmastime. But the reality on Christmas morning was that most of us did not receive every item we requested. We all remember that one coveted thing that, for whatever reason, we just didn't get.

God has something for us that's much better than our Christmas wishes; Scripture is full of *promises*. From Genesis to Revelation, the Bible offers more than three thousand promises God made to His people—and there is no need to decide which things we *really* want. He will not randomly choose which promises to keep. All of God's promises will be fulfilled; they all find their yes in Christ.

Whether in reference to His place of birth, His lineage, or His sacrificial death, Jesus is evidence that God keeps His promises. Jesus is also the fulfillment of every prophecy, and He is the answer to every prayer. In fact, Christmas offers evidence that God keeps His Word and that nothing is impossible for Him.

What is your heart's desire this Christmas? What is that thing that you are almost afraid to hope for? We all have something. Let's trust God with it. Our prayers do not go out into the void but rather to our Father, who loves us and cares for us. Let's leave the matter to Him, knowing that He desires what's best for us and that He answers every prayer in His time and in His way.

You are so faithful to us, Lord. You are true to Your Word. Help us trust You with our hearts' desires this Christmas. Amen.

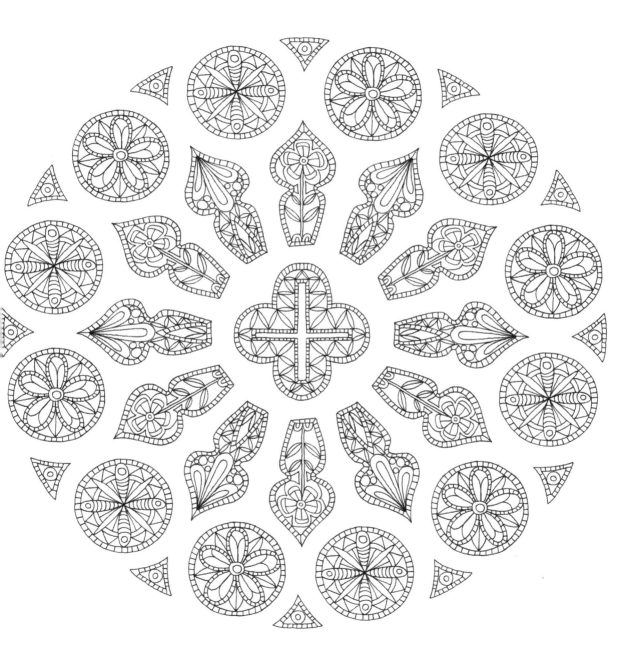

And Mary said: "My soul magnifies the Lord,

And my spirit has rejoiced in God my Savior.

For He has regarded the lowly state of His maidservant;

For behold, henceforth all generations will call me

blessed For He who is mighty

has done great things for me, And holy is His name.

And His MERCY is on those who fear Him

From generation to generation."

—Luke 1:46–50 nkjv

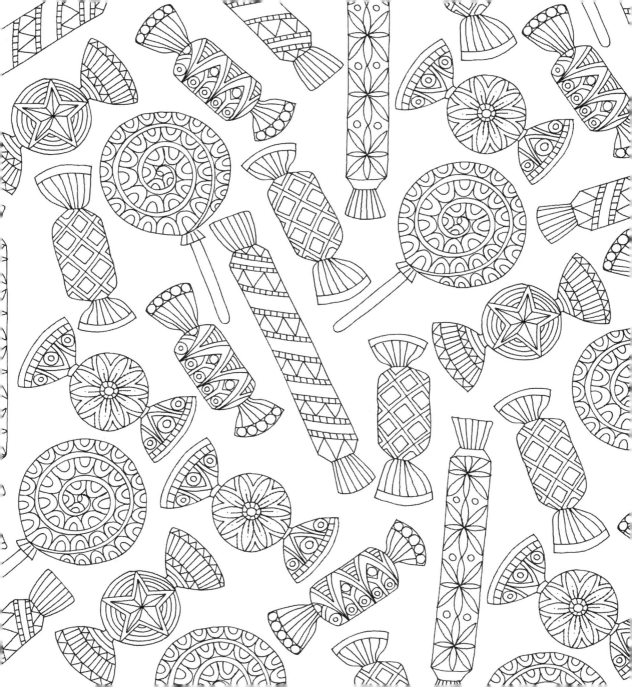

Holiday Memories

Mary treasured up all of these things, pondering them in her heart.
—LUKE 2:19

What is your favorite Christmas ornament? What or whom does it remind you of? The most loved ornaments usually carry special memories. They are the angels our grandmothers crocheted or the stars our children made from Popsicle sticks. One of the best parts of Christmas is taking the decorations out of their storage containers and, one by one, reliving the sweet memories we have treasured up over the years. Mary also stored up sweet memories from the day that Jesus was born.

The excited shepherds hurried to the manger immediately following the angels' visit in the field. After they had seen the baby, Luke reported, the shepherds shared the news, and all who heard it wondered at what the shepherds said. But back at the manger, Mary thought about all the shepherds had said about the angel's appearance and the multitude of heaven's army praising God. Mary pondered these things in her heart. While the shepherds bustled with excitement, Mary gathered her memories.

Christmas can be a hectic time for many of us. We get caught up in cooking, shopping, wrapping, and all the festivities. We hurry from one activity to another and, if we aren't careful, end up exhausted and empty at the end. Let's do it differently this year. Instead of scurrying around, let's look around. Let's take note of the children's giggles and smile at Grandpa napping in the chair. Let's leave the dirty dishes and instead sit with loved ones, sharing stories. Years from now, these memories will be the treasures that we cherish time and time again.

Help us treasure up what matters, Lord. Teach us the value of memories over material things. Amen.

Real Christmas Trees

"This people honors me with their lips, but their heart is far from me."
—MATTHEW 15:8

Artificial Christmas trees date all the way back to the 1800s. It wasn't until the 1960s and the introduction of the aluminum tree that they became popular in the United States. Was the Christmas tree of your childhood a prickly artificial tree or a fragrant, sticky, real one?

The artificial trees of today are becoming more and more realistic. Unlike the shiny, silver ones of the '60s, today's artificial trees are designed to look just like the real thing. Many of us have been fooled into thinking that what stood in someone's living room was a live tree—and it wasn't. The true test to determine a live tree from an artificial one is if you're still picking up pine needles in February.

The true test for Christ-followers is the condition of our hearts. During Jesus' time on earth, He had faithful followers and angry opponents, including the Pharisees, a group we might call "the artificial faithful." They looked the part and played the part. If we had seen them in a crowd, we may have been fooled into thinking they were the real thing, but they were putting on a show. Christ was never fooled because their selfish hearts always gave them away.

Christ is never fooled by us either. We are as different as the Christmas trees in our living rooms. We have different gifts, and we have different struggles. Through it all, God sees our hearts and is able to judge what about our faith is real and what isn't. What matters is the condition of our hearts; God cares what's in them. This season, let's take time to reflect on our heart motives and make sure we are watering our faith and keeping it alive.

Examine our hearts, Lord. Show us any areas where we have been artificial in our dealings with You or with others. Amen.

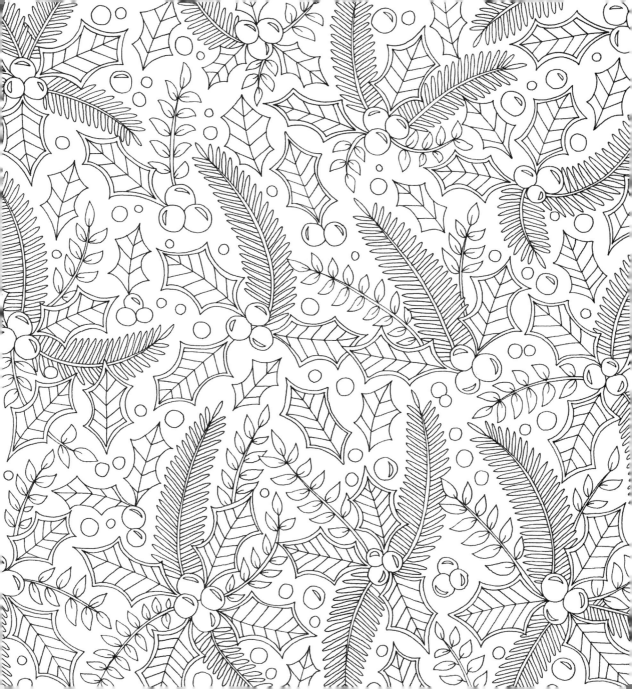

Joseph also went up from Galilee, from the town of Nazareth, to Judea, to the city of David, which is called Bethlehem, because he was of the house and lineage of David, to be registered with Mary, his betrothed, who was with child. And while they were there, the time came for her to give birth. And she gave birth to her firstborn SON and wrapped him in swaddling cloths and laid him in a MANGER, because there was no place for them in the inn.

—LUKE 2:3–7

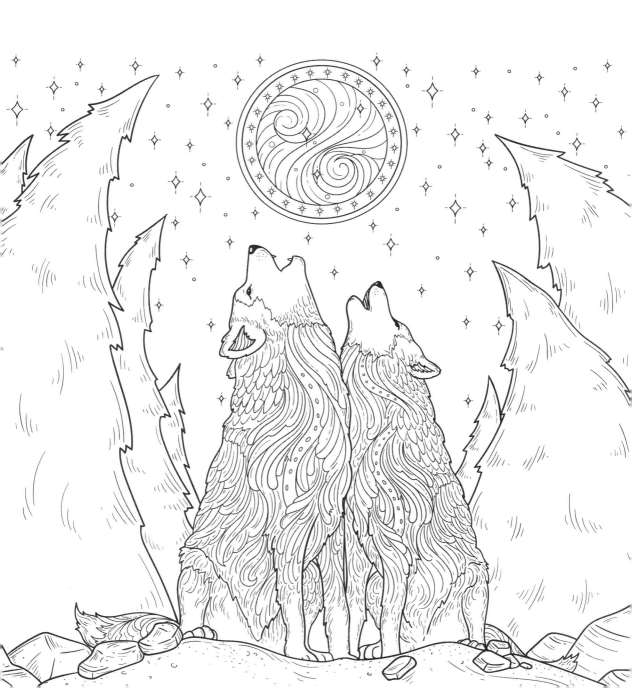

A Modest Christmas

*She gave birth to her firstborn son and wrapped him in swaddling cloths
and laid him in a manger, because there was no place for them in the inn.*
—LUKE 2:7

T he Little Drummer Boy" is a classic Christmas song written in 1941. It's about a little boy invited to see the Christ child. Being a poor boy, he's worried about not having a suitable gift for the newborn King. The little boy is far more concerned about this than Jesus is. Do you find yourself concerned in the same way this year? Have you been counting down the number of paychecks until Christmas? Are you disappointed that this may be a modest Christmas?

When God sent His Son into the world, the options were unlimited. He could have been born into a wealthy family who would have provided Him with a lavish lifestyle. He could have been raised in a bigger town with more prestige. Instead, Jesus was born to humble parents in humble circumstances.

Those very circumstances made the little drummer boy in the song feel as if he could approach Jesus. He visited the manger and declared, "I am a poor boy too." He connected with his Savior.

Some Christmases are more modest than others. Most of us have experienced lean years, and we might not have been able to see the beauty in them. But what if we didn't view a humble Christmas with disappointment? Whatever circumstances you find yourself in this year, don't let anything stop you from opening your heart to Jesus and to those around you.

The gift of Christ is truly priceless, and it is ours! A lavish Christmas celebration is not what matters. What counts is our humble worship of the King. Jesus accepts our praise no matter how "poor" we may consider it.

Thank You, Lord Jesus, for entering our world in such a humble way. Thank You, God, for that first modest Christmas at the manger—and for giving us a gift of infinite value. Amen.

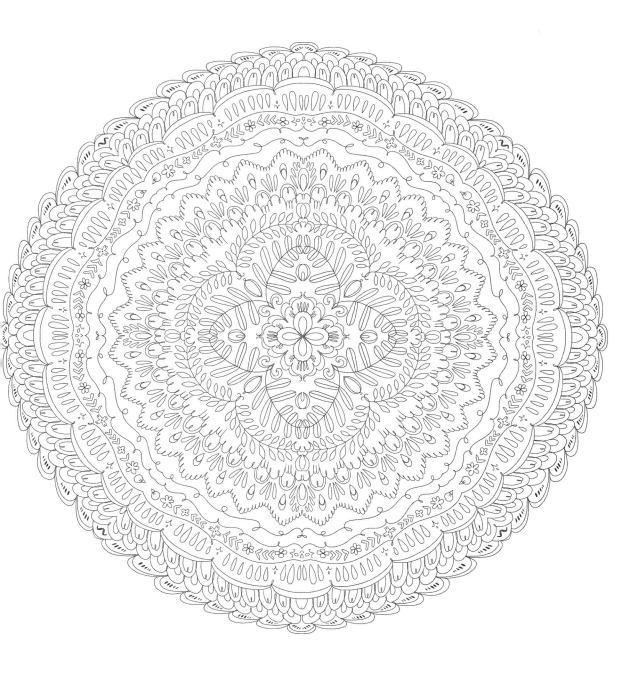

Dropping Hints of Hope

The Lord GOD does nothing without revealing his secret to his servants the prophets.
—AMOS 3:7

How good are you at keeping a surprise a secret? Can you keep it to the very end, or are you the type who drops hints in the hope that the surprise will be discovered? We all know that person who nearly bursts at the seams when trying to hold something in—and some of us are that person! From unexpected gifts to surprise guests, Christmas is a season of fun secrets.

Scripture shows us that God drops hints. In fact, for those willing to listen, He shares His plan outright. Isn't there something warm and endearing about God wanting to share details about His Son? Throughout the years He was whispering pieces of His plan to the prophets.

In the book of Jeremiah, God saw His people wandering in the darkness and whispered, "Don't give up. He's coming." God told Isaiah about the virgin birth. It's as if He just couldn't help but give hints about what was to come. God knew He had the perfect gift to give to the world, and He wanted to prepare His people for its delivery. Because of these holy whispers throughout history, believers were expecting Christ.

Still, there's much we don't know about the ways of God. Yet because of Christmas, His love for us is no secret. His hints offered in the Scriptures were fulfilled in the manger. And He continues to whisper good things to His children: "For I know the plans I have for you . . . plans for welfare and not for evil, to give you a future and a hope" (Jeremiah 29:11). May we tune our hearts to listen for God so that we do not miss any secrets He may whisper to us this season.

You are such a good Father. You reveal great things that bring our hearts comfort and joy. Amen.

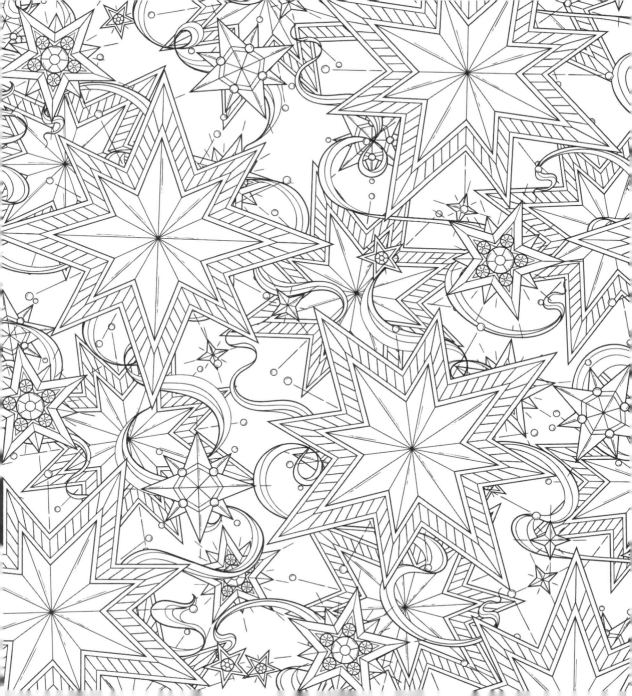

Suddenly there was with the angel a multitude of the HEAVENLY host praising God and saying: "GLORY TO GOD in the highest, And on earth peace, *goodwill* toward men!" So it was, when the angels had gone away from them into heaven, that the shepherds said to one another, "Let us now go to BETHLEHEM and see this thing that has come to pass, which the Lord has made known to us." And they came with haste and found Mary and Joseph, and the BABE lying in a manger.

—LUKE 2:13–16 NKJV

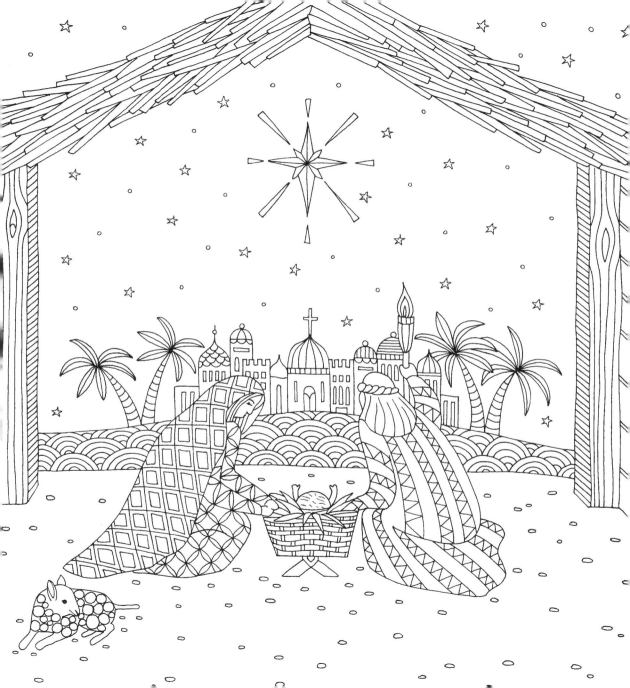

Christmas Jammies

Nicodemus said to him, "How can a man be born when he is old?"
—JOHN 3:4

Are you familiar with the Holderness family? They became an Internet sensation by making videos about their new Christmas jammies. Dressed in fuzzy snowman-covered pj's, they sing clever lyrics about their family Christmas traditions as they dance around. Folks are hooked, because who doesn't love a grown man and woman wearing footed pajamas? The fabulous part is that these hilarious garments come in all sizes—because no one is too old or too big for Christmas pajamas.

Something about Christmas seems to make us young again. We can't help but experience at least a little childlike wonder this time of year. How sad it would be if we felt too old to throw a snowball or build a gingerbread house! Christ's love embraces all ages.

You may know of Nicodemus. He was an old man, familiar with Jesus' teaching and wanting to know more. As he talked to Jesus, Nicodemus asked, "How could it be possible for someone to be born again to see the kingdom of God?" This troubled Nicodemus because he was already old: his birth had happened a long time ago.

Jesus gave Nicodemus—and us—good news: we are never too old to choose God and be born of the Spirit. The Spirit of God makes us new and enables us to have a childlike, trusting faith. Furthermore, as long as there is breath in our bodies, God can use us. It's not too late. We have not missed our chance to make a difference in the world. There is no limit to what God can accomplish through a willing vessel. We are not too old for God to use—and we're not too old for Christmas jammies!

Use us, Lord. We may have the bodies of adults, but give us the faith of a child. Amen.

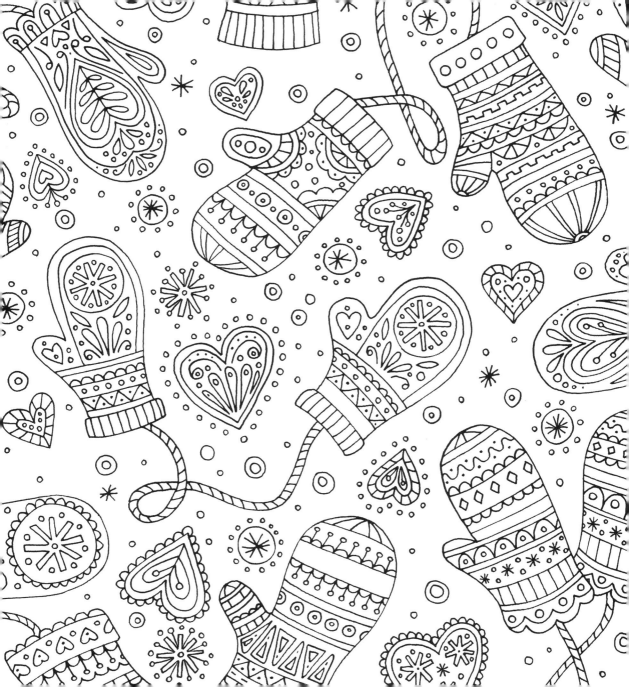

Christmas Stockings

"Call to me and I will answer you, and will tell you
great and hidden things that you have not known."
—JEREMIAH 33:3

Have you ever hidden a special gift deep inside the toe of a child's Christmas stocking? It's exciting to watch that child pull out candy and trinkets when you know something precious is waiting! And it's frustrating when the child is satisfied with the candy and doesn't dig deeper. *Will this child ever dig for the greater prize?* you wonder.

Do you ever feel as though your life is missing something? So many of us have gratefully accepted Christ as Savior, but we have not gone any deeper in our relationship with Him. We love Jesus, but as we meet the challenges of everyday life, we stop searching for Him. We forget God has things yet to reveal. We are missing out on an important gift: more of Him.

Yes, there is a sweetness to salvation, much like the chocolate treats at the top of the stocking. We should certainly embrace and enjoy that indescribable gift—but let's also go deeper! We will miss out on gems of wisdom, gifts of strong character, and the hope that comes as a result of perseverance unless we are willing to go further with Christ.

The writer of Hebrews said that we must come to God believing that He exists *and* that He has rewards for those who diligently seek Him (Hebrews 11:6.) God is encouraging us to dig for the deeper gifts of Christ—to continue to pray, study, and serve Him. This Christmas, let's ask God to reveal to us the hidden treasures that we do not even realize are ours for the taking. He is waiting for us to seek the greatest prize—Him.

We long to know You more, Lord. Teach us the great and hidden things that are deep within Your heart. Amen.

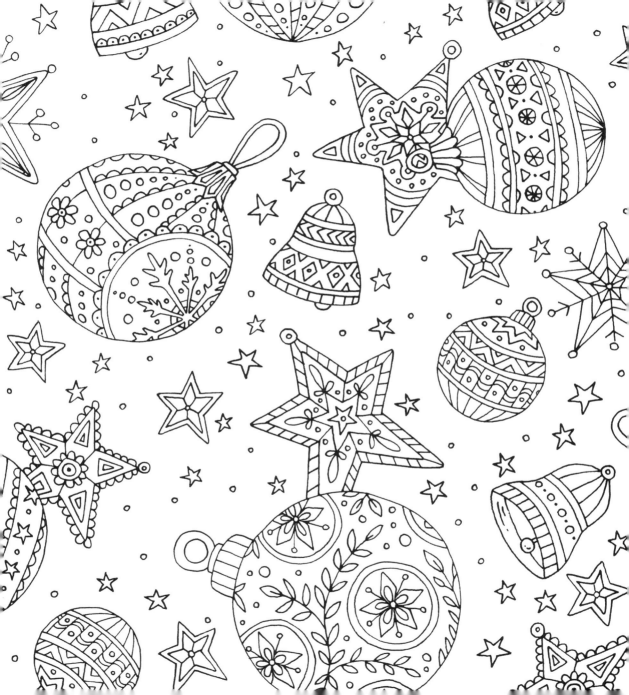

And the Word became

flesh

and dwelt among us,

and we have seen his

glory,

glory as of the

only Son from the

FATHER,

full of grace and truth.

—JOHN 1:14

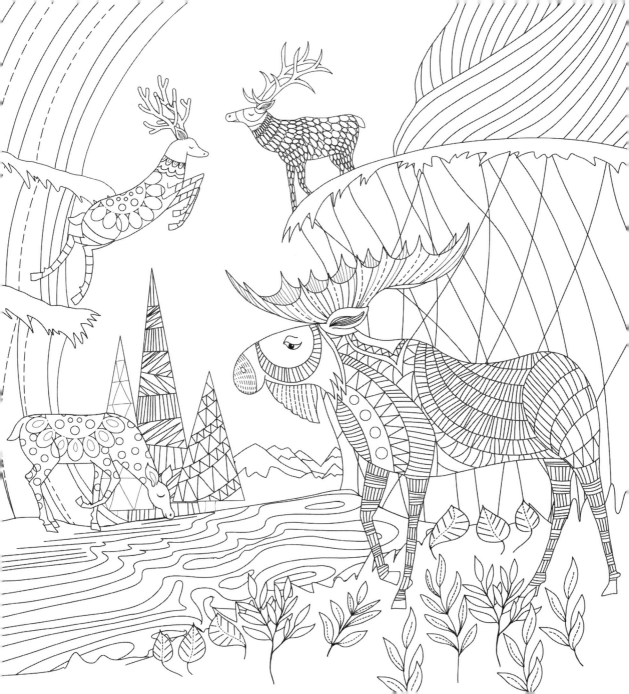

Gift Tags

"See, I have written your name on the palms of my hands."
—ISAIAH 49:16 NLT

How do you wrap your Christmas presents? There are so many options! Some people prefer wrapping paper decorated with cartoon characters or snowmen, and they add a nice peel-and-stick bow. Other wrappers choose shiny foil paper and tie an elaborate bow. Then there are those of us who begin with visions of beautifully wrapped packages but, somewhere around the twentieth present, pull out the gift bags and tissue paper.

Whatever presentation you choose, the last step is attaching the gift tag. You lovingly write a person's name on the tag and set the gift apart for that specific individual. It's the very last step in the whole process of thinking about, shopping for, and purchasing just the right gift. And when someone sees that gift sitting under the tree just for him or her, how special do you think that person feels?

God's love for His people is the most well-planned, extravagant gift of all time. He went to great lengths to prove His love to us. Then, lest there be any question, Jesus tells His people that their names are engraved upon His holy hands. The gift of God's love—Jesus, our Savior—has our names written on it. He is ours to receive.

It would be terribly sad for such a precious gift to remain unopened, but the Enemy would have us believe that God's gift isn't for us. He tells us we are unworthy of God's love. Do not believe it, dear one. Through His Son's sacrificial death as payment for our sins, God has made us worthy. Jesus' hands are marked with our names so we know that the gift of Christ is for us.

It's heartwarming to see our names on a gift tag, knowing that someone thought so much of us. Yet, no earthly gift compares to knowing that our names are written on Your hands and on Your heart. Thank You, Lord, for giving Your Son to us. Amen.

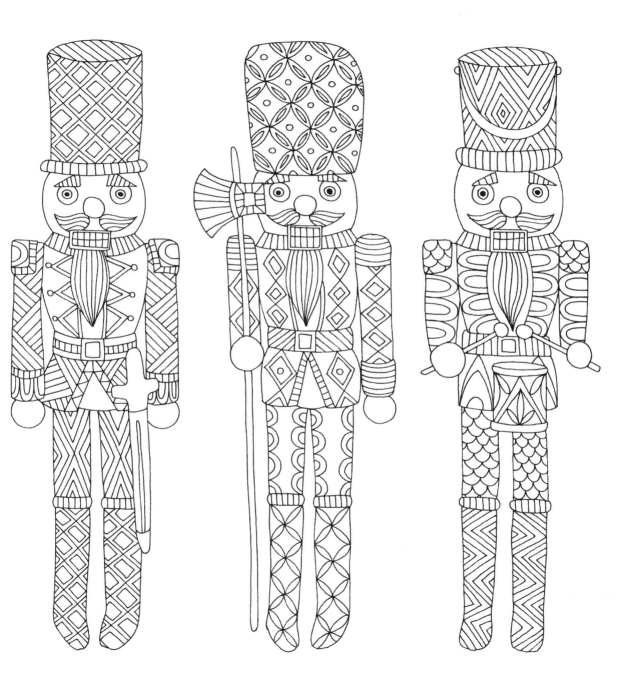

Christmas Letters

There is one mediator between God and men, the man
Christ Jesus, who gave himself as a ransom for all.
—1 Timothy 2:5–6

A couple of weeks before Christmas, many of us start to walk to our mailboxes with expectation. We know that Christmas cards and letters will arrive almost daily. Families in matching outfits will grace the covers of glossy cards. There will be postcards with brief greetings. Then there are the Christmas letters, replete with details of the past year. Whose Christmas letter do you look forward to receiving?

Christmas letters are personal things. They don't go to everyone because the message isn't for everyone. Not everyone needs to know that you've decided to go back to your natural hair color or that your little sister finally got her braces taken off. These letters contain a specific message for specific people. To share someone's letter with an unintended recipient might even amount to gossip.

While some Christmas letters may not be for everyone, the story of Christmas absolutely is for every single one of us. Christ came to earth because God loved the whole world (John 3:16). Anyone reading Scripture can be confident that the message is meant for him or her. Christ came for everyone, and He died for everyone. In today's verse, Paul wrote that Christ gave Himself as a ransom for all.

It's easy to assume that everyone knows the message of the gospel, but that's not the case. People we know hunger and thirst for the hope of Christ, and those of us who hold fast to the Word of God must be willing to share the truth on its pages. You may not want to share with the world the details in another person's Christmas letter, but the gospel isn't gossip. It's good news. Let's share it!

Your love is for everyone, Lord! You have made a way for everyone to come to You. Give us the boldness to share the gospel with the world. Amen.

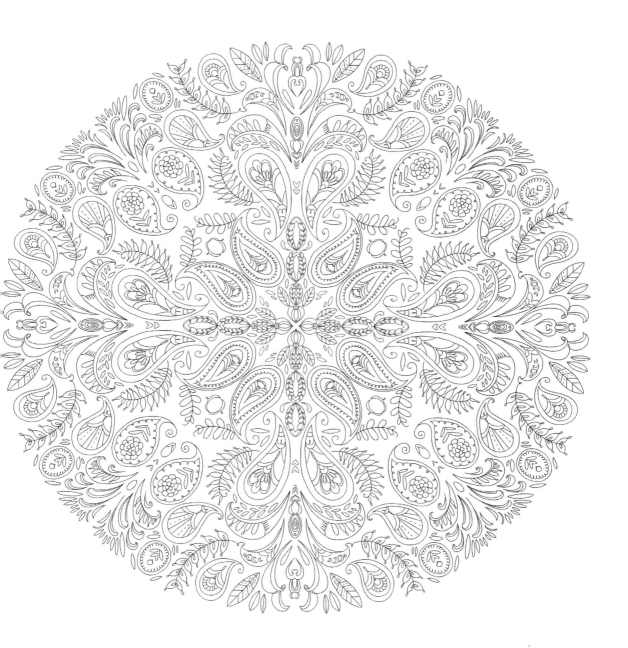

For God so *loved* the world, that he gave his only Son, that whoever BELIEVES in him should not perish but have *eternal* life.

—JOHN 3:16

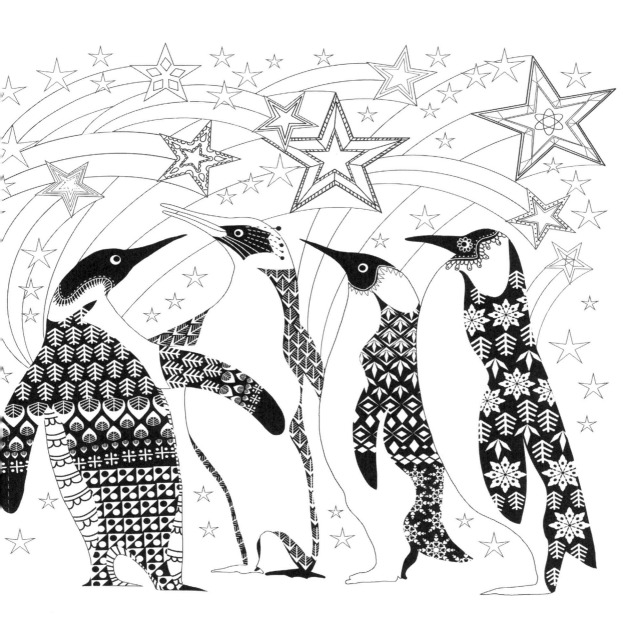

Going Caroling

*Coming up at that very hour [Anna] began to give thanks to God and to
speak of him to all who were waiting for the redemption of Jerusalem.*
—LUKE 2:38

Have you ever gone Christmas caroling in your neighborhood? Historically, caroling in England was a way of wishing one's neighbors good health, and it was not strictly a Christmas activity. It wasn't until the 1800s that Christmas carols made their way onto the song list. Caroling became a popular way to spread Christmas cheer to friends and neighbors. The joy of Christmas was shared with the whole community.

In the hours, days, and weeks after Jesus' birth, those people who learned about the baby Messiah were quick to share the good news with those around them. The shepherds who went immediately to the manger told Mary and Joseph everything the angel had spoken about the Christ child (Luke 2:17)—and, after seeing the baby, the shepherds told everyone they saw about Him. Upon seeing Jesus in the temple, the prophetess Anna also told everyone about Him (Luke 2:38). Anna and the shepherds grasped the importance of what was taking place and shared the news with others.

So why is caroling not as common these days? Are we too busy? Are we afraid it would be an imposition on others? What stops us from sharing the wonder of Christmas with those around us? The important part is not the singing but the going.

What can we do to take the message of the Messiah to our neighbors? After more than two thousand years, the good news is still good news. People still need to know that the Savior has come for them. You can sing to your neighbors if you like, or you could take a casserole or invite them to a get-together. It doesn't matter what methods we use as long as we share the message of Christmas in our communities.

Lord, Your birth is still worth celebrating and sharing. Help us to take to those around us the good news of Your coming. Amen.

Holy Anticipation

*It had been revealed to [Simeon] by the Holy Spirit that
he would not die before he had seen the Lord's Messiah.*
—LUKE 2:26 NIV

Is there anything more exciting than Christmas Eve? Family and friends will soon be filling our homes with love and laughter. The presents that we have lovingly chosen and wrapped will finally be opened. All of our planning and preparation has brought us here, and now we wait with anticipation.

Simeon was no stranger to anticipation. The Holy Spirit had promised Simeon that he would not die before seeing the Christ. He might have woken up each morning thinking, *Today could be the day!* Every day Simeon continued to draw breath, he waited to see the promised Messiah. That, my friend, is a life filled to the brim with anticipation.

Just as Simeon longed for Jesus' coming, we now long for Him to come again. We see promises of His return all throughout Scripture. The book of Revelation tells us that He is currently on His way, bringing justice and a new world (22:12). We live with the knowledge that not only will He come someday but that He could come *any day*. How exciting is that?

For those of us who long for Jesus' appearing, our days are filled with anticipation and significance. A day is no longer just another twenty-four-hour period filled with tasks to do and errands to run. Every day—any day—could be the day of Jesus' coming. And that possibility means that, for us, every night can be like Christmas Eve. Let's greet each new day with great anticipation knowing that Jesus could arrive at any moment.

It is with great anticipation, Lord, that we await Your return. May we live in such a way that when You arrive, we can say, "Yes, Lord, we were expecting You." Amen.

When the FULLNESS

of TIME had come, God sent

forth his Son, born of a woman, born

under the law, to REDEEM those

who were under the law, that we might

receive adoption as sons.

—GALATIANS 4:4–5

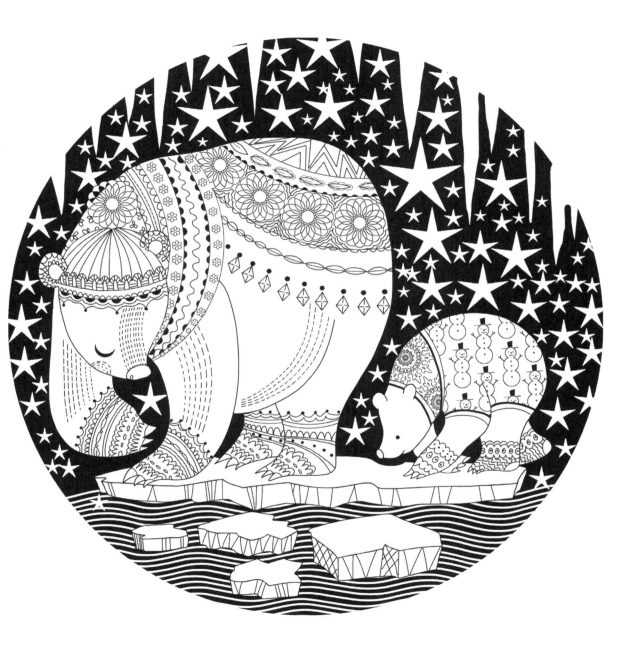

A Savior Is Born for You

Today a Savior, who is Messiah the Lord, was born for you in the city of David.
—LUKE 2:11 HCSB

Would it surprise you to know that December 25 probably isn't the exact day of Jesus' birth? Many Orthodox Christians, whose churches never adopted the Gregorian calendar, celebrate Christmas on January 7.

And what about the year of Jesus' birth? Would it shock you to know that many biblical scholars believe Christ was born between 6 BC and 4 BC? We simply do not know the exact date that the angel declared, "Today a Savior . . . was born." But that isn't the most important part of the message.

Whether today ends up being a wonderful day, or if it doesn't end up as you hoped it would, the events of *today* are not the most important part of the Christmas celebration. Wherever today finds you, the message is still the same: Messiah the Lord was born *for you*! What a life-altering fact! Jesus did not come to give us a sweet story to tell. He did not come so that we could have a reason to exchange gifts. Christmas Day is about God giving the gift of His Son to you so that you could belong to Him.

The gift is the same whether you are surrounded by family or sitting alone in your living room. The gift is as valuable on January 7 as it is on December 25. In fact, not knowing the exact date of Christ's birth may be a gift in itself. We do not have to limit our adoration to just one day! A Savior was born for us, and that truth is worth celebrating any day. Today, let us commit to celebrating God's gift each day of the year.

So much about You, God, remains a mystery. But knowing You sent Jesus to save us is enough. Thank You for the gift of Your precious Son. Amen.

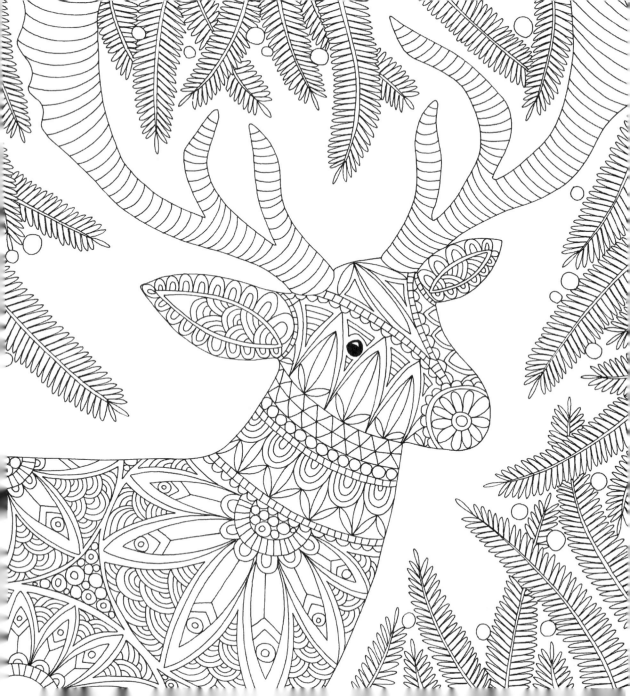

An Ugly Christmas Sweater

Every good gift and every perfect gift is from above.
—James 1:17

After weeks of fighting crowds and standing in lines, most of us are tired of being in stores. Yet—according to a *Wall Street Journal* article—in the days following Christmas, hundreds of us will flock to stores to return more than $60 billion worth of merchandise. What about you? Are you making plans to return an ugly sweater or that casserole dish you know you'll never use? Did you have gift receipts for your friends and loved ones?

After all, some gifts just don't work out. No matter how hard we try, we don't always know what someone wants or needs or likes. We may think we have come up with the perfect present for someone, only to see that person standing in the return line, holding our gift. It's possible that our choices are not as perfect as we thought.

But God's gifts are different. He knows exactly what we need. The gifts He places in our lives are good and perfect, although He gives us things that we never would have asked for or sought. Yet, in the end, God's gifts to us are always exactly right for us.

Is there something God has placed in your life that you wouldn't mind returning? If so, you're not alone. We do not always understand His gifts. Your struggle or misfortune may seem like an ugly sweater that surely must have been intended for someone else. But God makes no mistakes. Whether a trial is a consequence of sin, a thorn from Satan, or even something straight from God's hand, we can trust that He will turn it into something good and perfect. Let's choose to accept what God allows to come our way, knowing that He will make something beautiful out of whatever we face.

When we do not understand Your gifts, Lord, give us the strength to trust Your heart. We thank You in advance for all of Your good and perfect gifts. Amen.

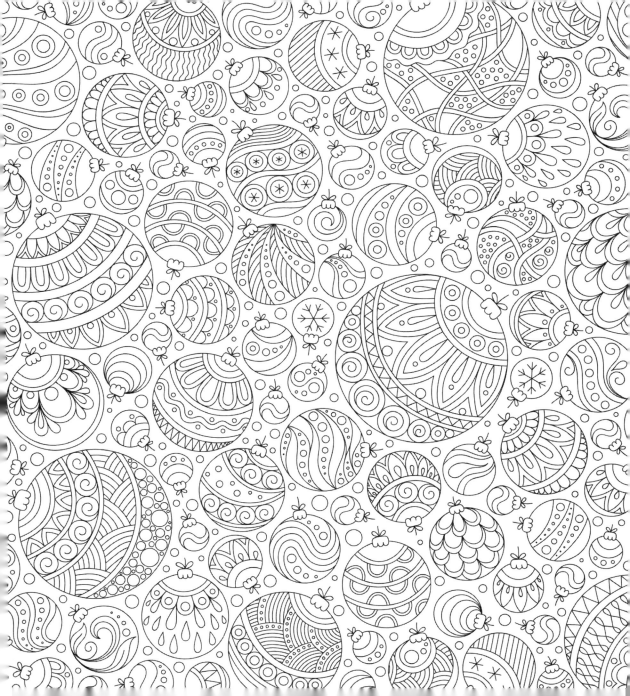

When the *kindness* and the love of God our Savior toward man appeared, not by works of righteousness which we have done, but according to His mercy He saved us, through the washing of regeneration and renewing of the Holy Spirit, whom He POURED out on us abundantly through Jesus Christ our Savior, that having been justified by His grace we should become heirs according to the hope of eternal life.

—Titus 3:4–7 NKJV

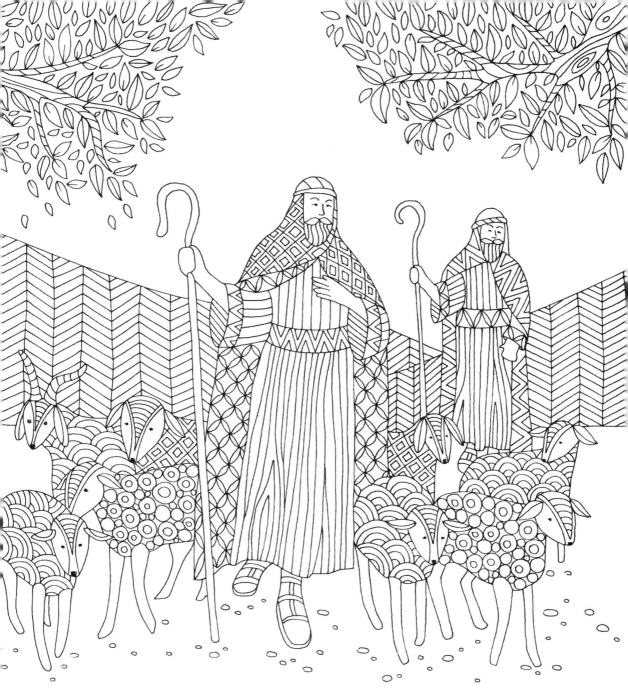

Christmas Leftovers

As for you, continue in what you have learned and firmly believed.
—2 Timothy 3:14 hcsb

Do you still have Christmas leftovers in your refrigerator? Not many things can beat leftover turkey and dressing—and eating leftovers is a way to keep the holidays going just a little while longer. Many people may have worked to create your Christmas meal, and you can relive that togetherness as you enjoy the containers full of delicious food.

Our spiritual lives are much like a Christmas dinner. At times, our loved ones surround us and pour into our lives. Other times we are alone, but we can return to the lessons they have taught us and continue to be blessed by them. Have you ever gone through a difficult season and been reminded of a Scripture verse someone taught you or a word of encouragement from the past? Those are spiritual leftovers, and they nourish the soul.

Paul warned Timothy that the day would come when people would begin falling away from the faith. Some would begin to doubt the things they had been told about Christ. So in today's verse, Paul encouraged Timothy to continue on in what he had learned. When life became chaotic or confusing, Timothy could go back to what he knew to be true.

We live in a constantly changing world. People are challenging Christian beliefs, and some are redefining scriptural truths to make them more acceptable to the world. But we do not need to repackage or reheat the Word of God, "for the word of God is alive and active. Sharper than any double-edged sword, it penetrates even to dividing soul and spirit, joints and marrow; it judges the thoughts and attitudes of the heart" (Hebrews 4:12 niv). The message of God's Word continues to be fresh and life-giving, perfect and true.

There is nothing new that can compare to You, Lord. No new philosophy can explain or encourage us the way You can. Help us to continue in what we have learned and firmly believe to be true. Amen.

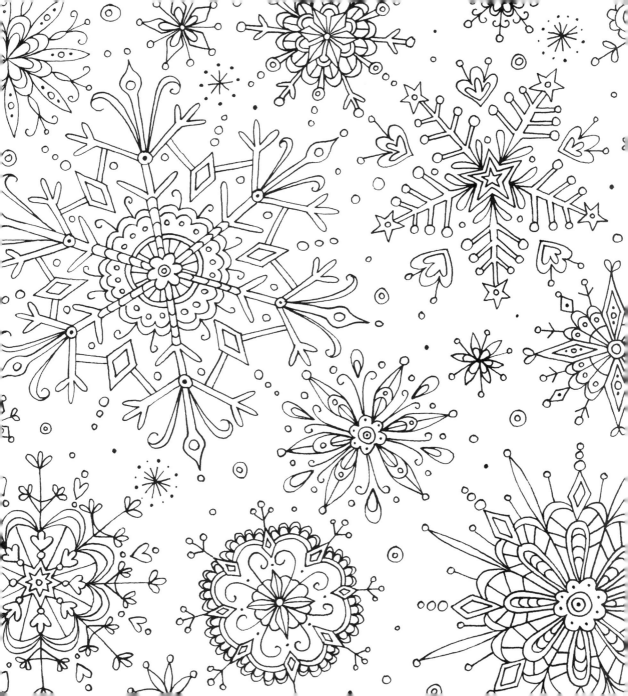

The Season Continues

Going into the house, they saw the child with Mary
his mother, and they fell down and worshiped him.
—MATTHEW 2:11

You may have seen a nativity set with three wise men standing right next to the shepherds in the stable. You may have one on your hearth right now, or perhaps the children at church acted out the Christmas story. This beautiful scene is ingrained on our collective memory. So while biblical scholars may not have been surprised, most of us were shocked to learn the wise men were not present at the manger. Now, before removing the wise men from Grandma's favorite nativity, let's think for a moment.

From Scripture we can surmise that it could have taken the unknown number of magi as long as two years to travel from where they were to where Christ was residing. They would have traveled by caravan and occasionally stopped for lodging. Everyone making the journey would have been very much aware that the goal was reaching the Christ child.

Today's Scripture tells us that immediately upon entering the home (not the stable), the magi fell down to worship Jesus. He was the reason—the only reason—they had made the trip. After worshipping Him, they presented the child with gifts. They were celebrating the birth of the Savior even though He had been born two years earlier.

It's common to feel a little bit of an emotional letdown following Christmas. So much effort and energy go into the weeks leading up to it, and then it's suddenly all over. But what if Christmas continued after the decorations were packed away and the leftovers were eaten? Let's linger over the Christ child a little longer. It is never the wrong time to celebrate the birth of Christ.

Lord, You are worthy of much celebration. May we honor and worship You not just at Christmastime but always. Amen.

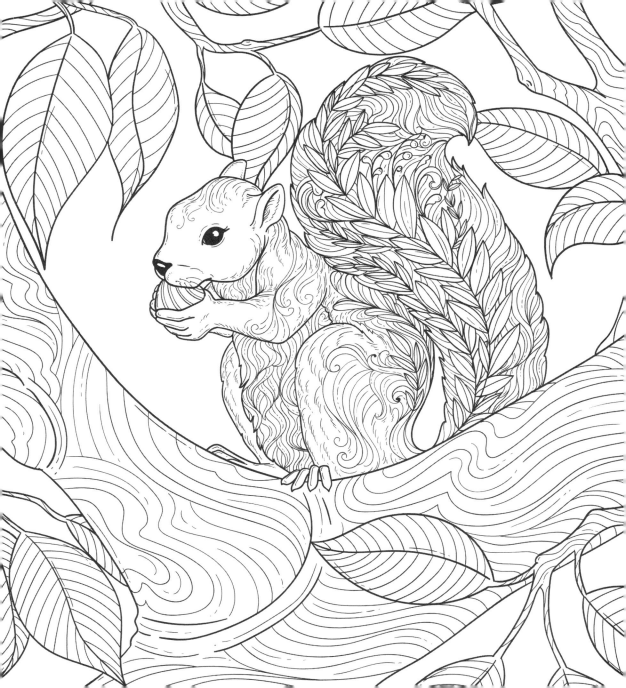

This is the

testimony,

that God gave us

ETERNAL life,

and this life is

in his SON.

—1 JOHN 5:11

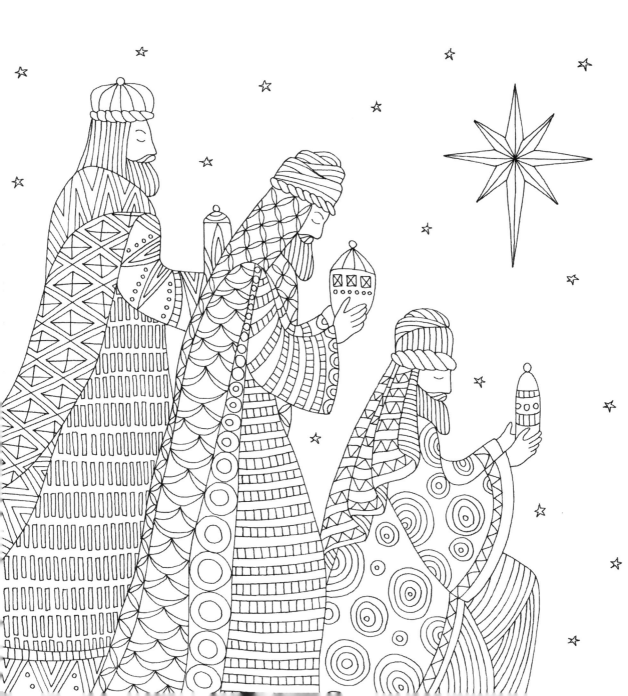

The Aroma of Christmas

We are the aroma of Christ to God.
—2 Corinthians 2:15

At Christmastime candles are popular in homes. Fragrances help create a warm, cozy atmosphere as well as happy memories. Candles come in delicious holiday scents like sugar cookie, cinnamon, pumpkin spice, and pine. One company sells a candle called "Christmas Eve." It smells like candied fruit. It smells good enough to eat!

American poet Diane Ackerman once said, "Nothing is more memorable than a smell." Furthermore, nothing about God's creation is accidental. He designed our bodies so the sense of smell is linked to our memories. Perhaps that is why Paul used the phrase "the aroma of Christ" to tell us that we are to be like a comforting scent in the memories of those we encounter.

Paul told the Corinthians that God uses believers to spread the fragrance of the knowledge of Christ everywhere. Then, in his very next sentence, he said that *we* are the aroma of Christ to God. In other words, we should always smell like Christ, leaving behind traces of His peace, His joy, and His grace. Have you ever known someone whose lovely scent lingers long after he or she has left the room? When we leave someone's presence, may Christ's scent—the essence of His holiness and love—linger.

Let's be intentional about the spiritual scent we leave behind. People will remember it. If we do everything as unto the Lord, everything we do should result in the lingering fragrance of Christ and reflect well on Him. Others should notice a sweet aroma when we interact with them. And when God draws near us, may we be living in such a way that He can't miss His Son in our lives. Throughout the year, let's share the aroma of Christmas.

There is no greater honor, Lord, than for our lives to radiate with the aroma of Christ. May the scent of our lives attract people to Your Son. Amen.

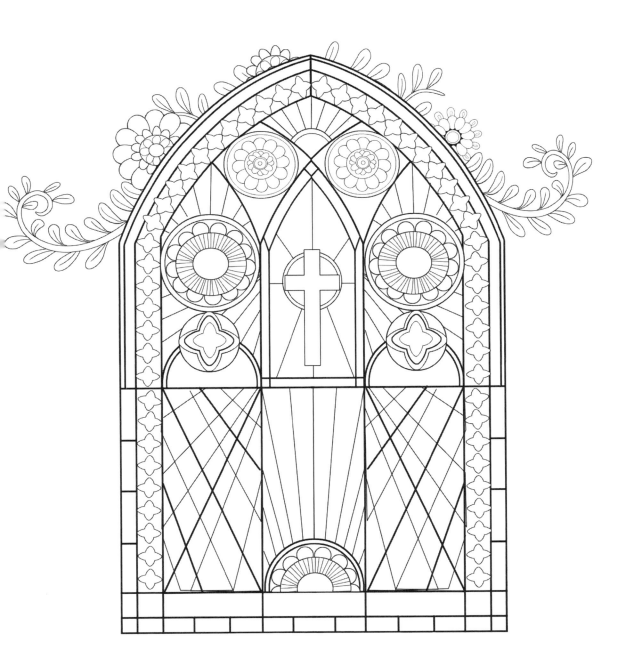

Cradle to Cross

*Then [Joseph of Arimathea] took [Jesus' body] down and
wrapped it in a linen shroud and laid him in a tomb.*
—LUKE 23:53

Things have a way of coming full circle. That's what we say about a situation that seems to end where it began. Can you think of a situation from your life that made you think things had come full circle? In the study of Scripture, we call this an *inclusion*. The book of Luke has several examples. Consider that the ministry of Jesus began with Satan in the wilderness, questioning His divinity (Luke 4:3), and Jesus' ministry ended with the rulers questioning His divinity as He hung on the cross (Luke 23:35). The very setting of Luke is an *inclusio*: the book opens and closes in the temple.

Think back to when Mary gave birth to Christ, wrapped Him in cloths, and laid Him in the manger. Imagine the gentleness of those hands as they held the Savior and the nervousness of a new mama as she laid Him in the manger. Now imagine Joseph of Arimathea as he removed Christ's body from the cross. Imagine the gentleness of those hands as they held the Savior and the nervousness of this believer's heart as he laid Jesus in the tomb.

The similarities between the way Mary and the way Joseph of Arimathea handled Christ's body are not coincidental. We are meant to link the cradle and the cross in our minds: they were always part of the same circle of events. One was intended to lead to the other. So, as we close out another calendar year and reflect on beginnings and endings, let's not lose sight of the fact that the baby in the manger became the Man on the cross. The end of His time on this earth—His resurrection from the dead—began a new beginning for the world and gave us new hope.

We have no adequate words, Lord, to thank You for Your life. Your birth, burial, and resurrection are gifts we treasure. Amen.

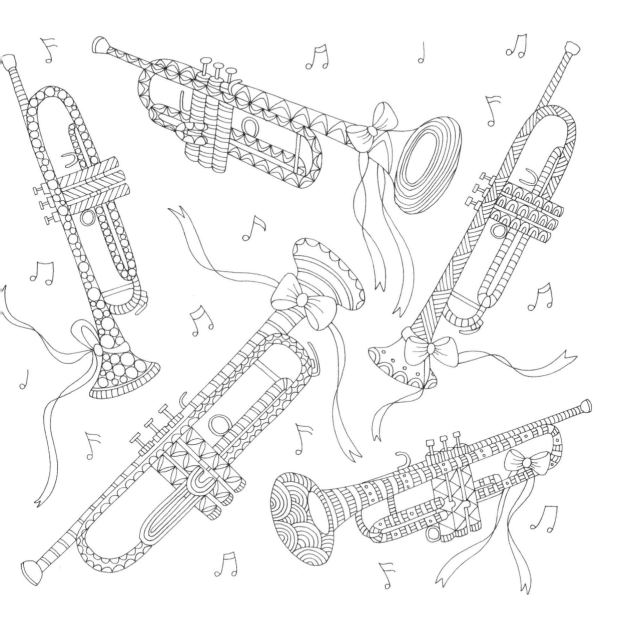

A New Thing

If anyone is in Christ, he is a new creation. The old
has passed away; behold, the new has come.
—2 CORINTHIANS 5:17

P ause and take a deep breath. You have made it through another Christmas season and are about to embark on a brand-new year. The gifts have been given, the holiday food has been eaten, and the decorations will soon be put away. (Some of us will not have the energy to take down the tree for a little while. That's okay. After all, Christmas is completely about grace.) For each of us, January is a time of new beginnings. What are you looking forward to in the New Year?

All throughout Scripture, Christ created new beginnings. A young virgin girl began the journey of motherhood. Prisoners began new lives of freedom, and the lame were given new hope through His healing. Jesus wiped away sins and sicknesses and offered people fresh starts. Could you use a new beginning?

How was this past year for you? Most of us could list a few highs and a few lows. We wish we could do some things over or perhaps not have done other things at all. But the good news is, Christ still delights in giving us new beginnings. We can move on from any mistakes we made this year. We can allow God to heal any wounds and lead us back toward Him. We can ask Him to begin a new work in us.

Let's not enter this New Year carrying old burdens. Wouldn't you rather have new blessings instead of old baggage? This is the perfect time to put down those burdens. Let the old pass away. In Christ, we are new creations created for new things. Prepare your heart to receive them.

Because of Christmas, Lord, we can be made new. Thank You, Jesus, that we are not just cleaned-up versions of our old selves but brand-new creations. Amen.

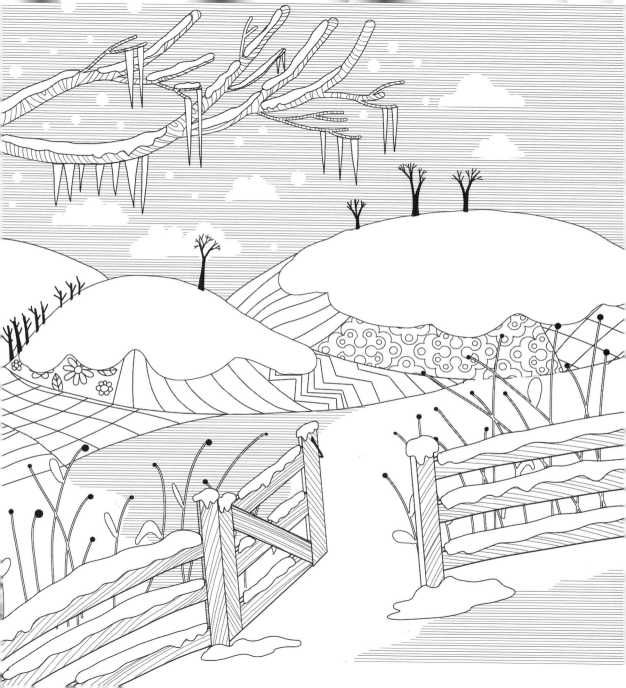

He who was seated on the throne said, "BEHOLD, I am making all things NEW." Also he said, "Write this down, for these words are trustworthy and true."

—REVELATION 21:5